What Keeps Me Sane

What Keeps Me Sane

Poems by

Esperanza Cintrón

Lotus Press
Detroit

First edition

International Standard Book Number: 978-0-9797509-7-0

Printed and manufactured in the United States of America

Lotus Press, Inc.
"Flower of a New Nile"
Post Office Box 21607
Detroit, Michigan 48221
www.lotuspress.org

To Annie and Otis
who made Patricia Smith
and to Ntozake Shange
who holds on to beauty even as she struggles

Preface

This collection began during a reading by Patricia Smith who read from her Annie and Otis series, which examines the lives of her parents before her birth. As I sat in the audience, I was so moved by her work that this cycle of poems began to form in my head. While this series explores the concept of sanity rather than relationships, the four women here are my Annie and Otis. Although a compilation of many women, they represent real lives, and all have impacted my perception of the world.

The first, Aiyo, whose name is derived from the Greek god, Aeolus, the Keeper of the Winds, and Ai, a cry of frustration, is a scribe, a griot, one who is charged with recording memory. Lily, a common flower whose natural beauty appears deceptively delicate is both enduring and perennial. Brisa, which means breeze or air in Spanish, reflects the prevailing carefree image of the islands. Yet, hurricanes begin with light winds and moist air. Plum, the last, is just that, a sweet, ripe fruit.

Aiyo, like Ntozake Shange and company, maintains the battle between truth and survival. Lily, the perpetual mother, bears the burden of complete sacrifice. Brisa, who is loosely based on my cousin, the Puerto Rican poet, Angelamaría Dávila, is the revolutionary giving her all to the cause, and Plum is a battered girl-child struggling toward the light.

Working with Naomi Long Madgett to bring this collection to print has been a journey. It was great having someone of her stature read my work so closely. There were discussions and debates about punctuation versus the use of white space, onomatopoeia, line breaks, and the African disaspora. I found many of her questions useful in making my final edits. Moreover, her title suggestions were much better than mine.

vii

Definitions

San•i•ty [san-i-tee] *noun* Middle English *sanite*, from Anglo-French s*anité*, from Latin *sanitat-*, *sanitas* health, *sanus* healthy; first usage 15th century. 1. the state of being sane; soundness of mind. 2. soundness of judgment. 3. the ability to predict the result of one's actions. 4. acting in one's best interest. 5. getting what you need without doing things that will get you more of what you don't need. *Synonymous to* wit, lucidity, reason, rationality. *Favorable characteristics* 1. the ability to function. 2. to carry out normal tasks. 3. to exist without hampering others. WORD ON THE NET IS that *sanity* is the free flow of the 7th chakra, which connects us to the Divine. It is located at the crown of the head and symbolizes the highest state of enlightenment. It is the cosmic consciousness that creates our belief system and controls our thoughts and actions. Some say it is violet, some say white; others swear it's multicolored. WORD ON THE STREET IS that it's about being able to pay your rent. If you don't have a place to stay, it's about standing up straight so cop cars will pass you by without tackling you to the ground and shoving you into a cell with no toilet seat and a bunch of strangers who lack *sanity*. MY SISTER SAYS *sanity* is a perceived reality, an individual's perception of normal. One act, one situation can tilt the scale. A POET FRIEND SAID that *sanity* is having enough sense to put on a coat when it's cold outside. She added that white people can't always tell when it's cold. MY DAUGHTER'S GODMOTHER SAYS *sanity* is happily complying with the norm or happily defying the norm. COUSIN SHAWNEE SAYS that *sanity* is being at peace, having a settled mind, the ability to focus. She says that when you see a homeless person talking to herself, what she's trying to do is achieve order. MY DAUGHTER SAYS that a *sane* person is someone who doesn't repeat an action if it doesn't work; a *sane* woman tries something different.

Contents

Aiyo

a composer of words

Aiyo (Ah-ee-yo)

1

Mother who called herself Osa
was all that is tranquil
and turbulent
The twins, Thandie and Tula,
younger than I
by more than a year
were her beloved calm
and I, she often said,
was her joy
one who bore the force
of the sun, the strength to
change our lives

2

Thandie, Tula and I dangled behind her
skipping and twirling
in sundresses and jeans
in pigtails and mop top curls
small bodies in big chairs
listening to loud talking poets
in dark cafes, to blues anthems
on grassy knolls, to droll novelists
who stretched up from behind wooden lecterns,
to animated musicians who plucked and blew
and banged their instruments from backlit stages
After the applause, we rose like a tide,
a woman with the gait and body of a dancer
and her three girls
Osa knew them all, tall men who bent down
to press smiles onto our fingers
and bright eyed women who stroked
our cheeks with warm hands
Thrusting me forward,
she beamed
This is my Aiyo
She is a composer
of words

3

When you were born,
Osa breathed
the mantra at breakfast
a prayer before bed
a whisper that still
whistles through my head
A caul of gold
blanketed your body
Your lashes sparkled so
and you did not cry
until the nurses
peeled it away
As a child, I touched the smile
that followed the words
and did all I could
to keep it there
While Thandie and Tula
jumped rope and sang *Mary Mack*, I
sat on the stoop
capturing their images in script
reworking and refining the words
until they sang and Osa glowed

4

Bashful, I stood
before the lowered microphone
murmuring the words
Dark voices from beyond
the lights laughed,
Louder they called
I froze
Then Osa said,
Speak up baby
and I could hear her smile
So I spoke the words for her
knowing that her arms
would engulf me after the applause

5

It was like that for a while
hugs and applause
kisses and smiles
But there were dark days
when the words wouldn't come
when the pen bled scratches and scribbles
nonsense and fear
Biting my nails, I would close the door
and wait
Sometimes they came
like crabs crawling through debris riddled sand
bumping and scurrying around obstacles
Sometimes I would sit near the window
a shell discarded by its last occupant, hollow
Sometimes the pall lasted a day or two,
sometimes weeks
Osa brought sandwiches and juice,
sliding the tray onto the nightstand
She would stroke my head as though
testing for fever, her smile weak, forced

6

But when it was good, it was very good
Crisp volumes lined the shelves
A golden *Aiyo* carved into each spine
The podium firm beneath my elbows
Crowds with eyes brightly tilted up
who grinned and bobbed their heads
who stood, cheered and clapped
Thandie and Tula were well fed
and Osa smiled
as my pen sped across the page
capturing sounds and scenes and people
specimens placed in glass boxes
to be culled, pondered and displayed
pages and pages of images to dissect,
to be scraped clean and recarved, to last
to carry me through the next squall

7

Sometimes when I pinch my shin hard
it comes again, the flow of words
like a jolt, a stream of electricity
It works best if I squeeze
the soft tissue inside my arm
Long nails enhance the flow
like digging-in anchors the current
leaving tiny moon crescents
scythes of blood
easily covered by long sleeves
I have a number of them,
long sleeved sweaters
in assorted colors, pastels
to match the flirty sundresses
and wedge heeled sandals
for which I'm known

8

The last squall rent and roiled
longer than the one before
I could tell by Osa's face, the tightness
in her eyes, the way one flinched
when she grinned
Blue pills and long talks in a dim room
A freckled scalp that nodded
whenever I spoke
An expert on adolescents,
Osa assured me. He lasted
until blue merged with white
and yellow and green
The woman in the brightly lit room
wore white silky blouses with loose bows
A bay window behind her desk
looked out onto the shore
Having read my work, she was eager
to help. Osa assured me
She lasted until the din grew
blew pellets like hail and dead fish
slashing at the once bright glass
and an extended rest
in a proper facility
was prescribed
Not on Osa's watch.

9

She found another,
a thin man who
wore tunics beneath his white coat
whose long brown feet
rested cleanly in leather chappals.
He believed in the laying on of hands
the power of positive energy, herbs
and the right combination of drugs
Unsanctioned and unperturbed
the buccaneer medic nudged me
to the surface, prodding
until the words came
until the tick in Osa's eye
faded to a glimmer

10

But Osa, our strength,
was far frailer
than she appeared
Even the thin man
with the long bare feet
could not hold her here
Suddenly there were only
Thandie and Tula and me
and an ash filled urn propped against
a short row of tomes
with gold embossed letters on their spines

11

A quiet room
Bed, dresser, no mirror
a window set in scrolls of wrought iron
walls pale like the glare of the sun
on a limitless stretch of ocean
A numbing white covers
the inside of my eyes
When I speak
the wind blows my words away
They bob and trip across the fluttering swells
When others speak, their words are echoes
that glance off my ears
to bounce over the horizon

12

After a time,
the numbness fades
Absence becomes
a piercing prick of awareness
dragged down my torso
like a serrated knife
leaving me split open
entrails spilling out onto the sand
A flawed fish, discarded
Tears do not cleanse, they stain
The trail of salty particles burrows
leaving a mesh of scars, a net
to safeguard memory and substance
Pills, hard, like callused skin
tame the fears
and capture my voice,
holding it in my throat
like the flutter of a small fish
circling a narrow shoal.
I no longer recognize
the slow moist drag it has become
The echo of others has been distilled
into a low vibration
discerned only if one listens
with care
Sometimes the words flow
Sometimes I can skewer them with my pen
and mount them on the page

Lily

watched her future flicker and grow faint

Lily

Momma, you've been on my mind

1

The year she was born,
hungry veterans squatted
just beyond the green
lawns of the White House
A hasty village of unwashed faces
pressed against the wrought iron fence
as Hoover's red bellow
spewed tear gas and bayonets
And as the shanties burned
forty thousand Salvadoran peasants
remnants rising against another Cortés
were lured into a public square
and murdered
Hitler ran for President,
Shanghai exploded
and would be starlet Peggy Entwistle
dived off the H in Hollywood

2

The eldest of eighteen,
Lily was like her father
golden, fair, and well-made
She was her mother's treasure
until the others came
a procession of goslings
pecking through
and tumbling out
jostling for space
as their mother waddled
towards salvation
The fair Lily was left
a tag at the end of the line
to herd strays
and tend new hatchlings

3

Nearly a of score of them
lined up, huddled before the old stove,
all eyes on, oven door opened
A fresh kettle to add warmth
Each small hand waited
gripping the tin rim
as a cautious toe hovered, then dipped
She extended a water-wrinkled hand
pressed a thin shoulder down
a quick dunk. Water rose
slid over the slate gray sides of the tub
A dripping cloth sloshed
down grimy arms
up grubby legs
The water-wrinkled hand nudged
quick, lifted the slippery body out
dabbed it dry, slipped a nightie over its head
then swatted it off to bed. Babies are
God's bounty, according to the pastor
who was the only one, besides Daddy
who could make her mother smile
Mornings were an assembly line of
pony tails, braids, quick brushes and toast
coats, scarves, hankies and hats
Once the door whooshed closed
there were bottoms to swaddle
mush to make, burps to woo
and the late meal to lay
She couldn't wait to be gone

4

From the soft cushioned darkness
of the Psalms Theatre, she'd
been following the starlet
since she died in *Jane Eyre*
weighed down by life and bricks
forced to circle the square
mud squishing in her shoes
rain drenching her dark curls
the pale baby doll face wasted
Then she was
the girl who had everything
petticoated silk dresses and dainty heels
that clicked softly across marble floors
Her daddy held her, shielded her
but she fell for Fernando Lamas,
the gangster bad boy
She died again in Paris
a victim of frozen rain
and other people's selfishness
One summer they put her away,
wanted to slice off a piece of her brain
because she saw things too clearly
She should have played dumb
'cause Montgomery Cliff can't always
be there to save you
Still, she was feisty and fine
as a cat, and Lily wanted to be her
But Lily would have settled for being
Lena or Dorothy or even a Butterfly

5

The year she escaped
Bette Davis predicted
a bumpy ride
But broad shoulders
and strong arms beckoned
A shock of dark hair
one eye obscured. He grinned
a dimple, like Sam Cooke
She smiled back,
shielding her eyes
against the sun's white heat
the crowded beach
greedy gulls
and sniping children
His tongue was deliberate
measured, slowed by its music
His lips, warm and tropical
full like calypso, Belafonte's ruffled shirts
and Ricky Ricardo's conga
He was something else
something not home
She could be his Lucy
he could be hers
her man, her house, her babies

6

He turned out to be Anthony Quinn
in *Attila* or maybe
La Strada's cruel Zampanó
a lusty man who knew no faith
and had no allegiance
his dark looks a lure
for good times
with other women
The fights were loud
never failing
to wake their child
voices raised in heat
the crack and thump
of bottles thrown,
glass splintered
neighbors' broomsticks thudded
against ceilings
fists pounded walls
and grinning thick tongued men
his equally faithless friends
filled too small spaces
sprawling and winking
they grabbed and pinched
behind his back
mouthing obscenities
as stained fingers squashed stubs
ashtrays buried in burning butts
empty beer bottles strewn
across table tops,

rolled around the edges
of once clean floors
the blare of sirens,
a late night emergency room
White sheets and stainless steel
as a baby faced surgeon
tugged and stitched, tugged and stitched
at the gaping flesh of his stomach
trying to repair an angry husband's wrath
And then her mother died

7

Her father had died the year before
a victim of hard work and poor pay
There was no one else
The older ones who'd escaped
closed their eyes
and covered their ears
So Lily took the small ones in
There were still ten
with braids and brushes
toast and coats, and bottoms to swat
yet again
Zampanó found another red head
one who did as she was told
and had no children
to need her

8

She took moments, for herself
cautiously at first
having been taught to bear
the steadfast yoke of duty
that rewards awaited those
who sacrificed for the greater good
that deeds spoke for themselves
Not that she yearned for Christian spoils
but she feared retribution
and knew that young ones needed
care and a constant set of eyes
to monitor their path
a task she did with diligence
though she was young yet, and still fair
no more than six and twenty

Years blinked by
as panic sprouted
in narrow spaces
and crowded rooms
full of nattering, needy voices
endless errands, tasks, duties
A shroud of dependence settled
over her head, draping her shoulders,
a binding that grew ever tighter
She struggled, tugging at the veil
gasping for breath. She stole time
a morning here, an evening there
gathering desperate handfuls of sweet water

lifting them to her mouth. She drank
loud slurps and noisy swallows
but long droughts followed
and the pleasant taste of stolen moments
waned as she watched
her future flicker and grow faint
dimmed by the shadows of others

9

On weekends
she prowled used bookstores
gathering romance
and movie magazines like bouquets
The flirt at the bus stop
snatched her purse and ran
The truck driver from the diner
drank gin for breakfast
and whiskey at every other meal
The cop liked it rough
and had a roving eye
She couldn't trust him
around the girls
her sisters
only a few years younger
who railed against her rule
The cop came back one night
breathed the fumes of something foul
into her face and left her bruised
She hid the fist stained skin
under long sleeves and a scarf
he'd given her
shortly after they met
but she couldn't hide the purple eye
She had to take the glasses off sometime.

10

Now, when she grew nervous or scared
she bit the fat part of her palms
the greater the fear the harder the bite
What keeps me sane she began to chant
a silent ritual that resounded in her head
as she tried to think of something to savor
What keeps me sane she recited
as she crouched in the darkness
a small bundle of damaged flesh
cheek pressed to the chenille bedspread
knees clasped against her chest
Her teeth tested, gnawed
then sank into the rounded edge of her hand
What keeps me sane is the feel of slick paper
as I turn each sheet of glossy smoothness
and watch the color photos
 and shiny black   letters   stretch

across

the page

11

She waited tables at a truck stop
and worried over the long hours
but the pressure of dentists' bills
ablaze in red, chilled rooms
with near frozen beds and mouths
to fill with more than bread
propelled her forth with nothing said
When a child hurled curses at her head
or raised a hand as though to strike
she held her breath, stilled her rage
and did as her mother might
fell on her knees and prayed
Long hoarse throated nights
of chapped hands and chafed shins
a ritual of words that appeased
but then the headaches came
and when strange men smiled at her
she clutched her purse
and muttered pleas
as though she were still on her knees
Words failed to quell the pain
an echo pulsing in her ears,
jabbing through her temples
like the split end of a crowbar
banging against a window
chilled fingers pressed and clutched,
but failed to ease
so she bit down
gripping the soft skin that lined her cheeks

pulling at the fragile membrane
teeth clenched, tearing
Her tongue worried the tattered flesh
soothed the rawness
scanned the intricate lines
until terrors receded
and calm approached

12

Scars form, thicken, turn white
a ridge of memory, a finger
in a page before she presses on

A brace of iron
girds her waist
curls her lips,
and tightens her eyes

Few knew
that steel spikes
shielded a soft heart
that time and duty had
ravaged such beauty

13

What keeps me sane is the sodden nub of dripping cloth
It sloshes down the rubbery flesh of arms and rounded bellies
while flattened palms and flexed fingers swat
tufts of evaporating suds
Baby laughs bounce off the wall and drift down
like parachutes on wet white tiles

What keeps me sane is the yellow corn
shiny cobs, nubby torpedoes boiling in the pot
They bounce and roil as the flames lick the blackened steel
Turn up the flame and they dance like the boys
who flatten cardboard boxes
against the concrete on street corners

What keeps me sane is the point of the needle
as it presses through thick layers of denim
piercing the thin film of thumb skin
a smear of bright blood
on the faded shredding threads of
a shattered knee

What keeps me sane is the wiggling body
narrow shoulders wedged between my knees
I part the thick waves, dense strands of dark hair
revealing clean lines of pink scalp
a narrow finger leaves oil and shiny trails
Fist winds tightly around the wooden handle
as bristles draw and stroke the billowing mass
before I weave a set of civilized ropes

What keeps me sane is the next need
the next tear that requires a tissue
the next bottom that wants swatting
the next set of stairs that have to be climbed

Brisa

*wore the mantle of revolution
like a nun's habit*

Brisa

para mi prima

1

There were two of them
brown babies, a boy and a girl, negritos
Basilio, the kingly one, sat like Buddha
floating on a slow moving current
head perpetually hidden in a book
But Brisa was light and energy
La malangita, they called her
a hard little body like the root
hurtling forth, a constant force at play
salty sweat dampening sweet floral playsuits
as she raised her arms
twirling, dancing to the rhythm of the clavé
or tumbling down verdant hills,
spilling out onto mounds of sand
high-pitched giggles riding her descent

2

Her father told her of the massacre
the students who opened their mouths
and swallowed the bullets of soldiers
He had been among them
one who fell, but did not die
one who ran, but had not faltered
He was Boricua and Brisa was his future
She sat at his knee and listened
She understood the sorrow
On quiet nights as the ancient rush
and rinse of ocean stroked the island shore
he sang tales of struggle
and whispered songs of sovereignty
as Brisa, eyelids drooping, rested
her cheek against his cotton clad shoulder

3

Red rules in secret
as the usurper runs scared
fear seeping from his pores
breath short as he cowers
impotent as the spirit of fidelity
tramples the cane and
spreads across the fields like la ortiga
fast and fierce. Its prickly nettles
secreting a venom that burns and claws
Barbed furrows creep into cities
creating walls around the neighboring isle
as campesinos reclaim The Pearl
promising the purge of healing
Yuquiyu sits atop his mountain
waiting for the clouds to clear

4

They surprised her at first
the surges of despair
that swept over her
Sudden cloying clouds of dust
obscuring sunlit days
crushing piragua stands
smearing the joy of cherry ice
and ocean breaths with oily
Vaseline encrusted fingers
Demons of doubt and unfounded fear
peeked knobby little heads out
of darkly hidden crevices
Barely in her teens
she pondered the source
welcoming her mother's dismissal,
Las hormonas. And her father's
boast, *An artist's temperament*
After a time, she learned
to press the goblins back
to tuck them neatly away
between the pleats of a skirt
or bury them in a shoe
to be crushed and held for a time
under the arch of a flexed foot
She committed herself
to the song, raised her placard higher
sought the enemy she knew
the one that could be fought
with speeches, pickets and bombs

One of the faithful, she struck back
keeping the minions of madness at bay
with revolutionary rigor

5

As a young woman, she attended university
rallied, marched and sang
wrote odes to those who'd fallen
read Julia and lamented her loss
drank coffee in cafés with men
who quoted Mao
and tucked Marx into
the back pockets of well-worn jeans
Basilio attended too
There he found his true calling,
women, marveling at the myriad
shapes, sounds and smells
They lay with him in the grass
on the commons
while he read
sweet words
toques de Neruda
besos de Martí
'Silio's long brown fingers
tickled their scalps
threaded through their hair
and he was happy
But Brisa only grew more strident
as her comrades were secreted away
to smolder in mainland prisons
The usurper was fighting back
plying the starving with grains of rice
and tins of condensed milk
drowning the rising tide of fidelity

6

She wore the mantle of revolution
like a nun's habit, but there were lovers
Heavy hands clutched her waist
gripped and fondled her bottom
tugged her along the fecund paths
of El Yunque and Old San Juan afternoons
peering into shop windows
fervent evening tussles on empty beaches
and leisurely mango mornings
of lust and Lenin in rumpled beds
Moments of bliss beyond compare
of delicate breathless showers
of warm sand beneath calloused feet
of thick green leaves, the ruby rich of maga trees
And then, like tripping over
the knobby husk of a protruding root
there were days of despair
Sometimes she lingered where she fell
eyes closed tight to ward off the minions
a veil of darkness threatening to consume her
as she cowered in once cozy corners
wearing stale pajamas, speaking to no one

7

When she surfaced,
there was always the cause
Letters to be written
calls to be made
fears to be soothed
solutions to be weighed
actions to be taken
a people to be saved
banners to be hung
and mantras sung
It caught her up on its lap
Free Lolita Lebrón
Stroking her with its sweeping balm
Fight imperialism
like the last winds of a tropical storm

8

A Borinquen beauty and bright
she was well liked and much praised
her words repeated and oft obeyed
Tireless and moored by her vision
she rarely drifted and never strayed
But once,
she stumbled into a harbor of respite
one who wore trim whiskers
in tribute to the hero of the Bolsheviks
His eyes smiled at her and she saw
all that she could be
His warm flesh calmed the restless island air
and kept the *gnarled witches* at bay
for a time
He baked because Lenin had valued bread
and esteemed cooks
So Brisa began to gather roots and tubers,
sweet potato, tannia, dasheen with
onion, garlic, cilantro and olive oil
She washed, chopped, minced
made salads with the green leaves
She boiled, simmered, baked, mashed
and deep-fried
Served up sizzling, steaming platters
They fed each other with greasy fingers
in the cramped confines of their nest
drank cool wine and spoke of Buddha babies
For a time, bliss reigned
until the doubt came, a blinding shroud of guilt

What right had she to joy when others suffered so
She fell, tumbling into the familiar darkness
foot wedged beneath the stiff knot of protruding root
The eyes of the Bolshevik dimmed
and he wrung his hands
as Brisa faded into the distance

9

She holds on
to the root
its thin rough skin
abrasive
but harmless
as it rasps against her palm
Therapy is slicing
the slight brown parchment
paring it away
until the milky meat is bared
Yucca, chopped and cubed
boiled in minced garlic
then simmered in an iron skillet
with onions and oil and salt
the marrow of existence

10

She struggles to the surface
her breath shallow and broken
Basilio reads to her
strokes her frail fingers
his warmth covering her ashen hand
The Bolshevik has fled to the mainland
Someone says he's gone to study Kafka at NYU
That makes Brisa laugh
the tenuous sound of ice cracking
Most days she lies in bed,
the white sheets pulled over her head
At night she sits by an open window
the smell of ripe earth and ocean wafting in
as her pencil rapidly darkens the page
Julia is long dead
Lolita is rotting in prison
Olga has escaped to Cuba
The Taíno are still enslaved
Oh night, sprinkled with stars
that send from all its luminaries
the purest harmony of reflection,
a nuptial offering to my thalamus![1]

---

[1] These last four lines are translations of a stanza from "Noche de amor en tres cantos" by Julia de Burgos. The original stanza reads, " Oh la noche regada de estrellas/ que enviará desde todos sus astros/ la más pura armonia de reflejos/ como ofrenda nupcial a mi tálamo!"

11

Pages fill with circles
stars and half moons
darkened with charcoal
lines, lines, lines and dashes
rushed little slashes that
crease and cut the vastness
Ovals like masks
with hairy eyes and
no mouths
shrinking and growing as
they march across the page
slipping down the margins
an eerie descent into nothing . . .
only to reappear at the top
again
beckoning
again
The velvety smoothness of the charcoal
like the cotton of her father's shirt
the warm dampness against her cheek
his salty smell
Fingers smudge her face
a smear of grit and tears
as she leans forward, nostrils flaring
Circles swell and contract
Lines vibrate like tuning forks
easing closer to dashes
The tip of her finger caresses them
marveling at their furred skin

at the soft haze that surrounds the circles
at the smiling eyes of the ovals
She strokes their brows then steps out
onto a sliver of coal moon as her fingers
reach and stretch towards a floating spray of tinsel

Plum

dropped from her momma's womb like a stone

Plum

for Rachel who survived,
Nettie who flourished anyway,
and so many others who didn't

1

Plum, purple, round and ripe
juicy like her namesake
like her momma
a shorn haired African beauty
born to a country stuck on Norse statues
Dropped from her momma's womb
like a stone, a burden to be dragged along
with the current of life
another chore, another hurdle
one more penalty for the sin
of being born
woman
black
and poor

2

Plum killed her daddy
early one morning with a hammer
while her mother was sleeping
but he wasn't
really her daddy
he was a guy her momma picked up
at a diner downtown one day
guapo smooth and dark eyed honeyed skin
just like her momma liked them
brought him home
opened the door
and he burrowed in
a stray rat grinning, bright eyes
in a fresh bed of food scraps
nestled in a battered but serviceable newspaper
made her momma happy like the sounds that rang out
from her bedroom, raucous and unrestrained
giggles and groans to the chorus of his accented baritone

3

He smiled at Plum with his greedy eyes
mouth always half open
ready for the next bite
eyes watching, waiting
for the unguarded crumb
fingers flexed and eager
He purred in her ear
a gnat, a fruit fly, an Asian beetle
ever present, no matter how she swatted it
Pretending goodness
he pursued
Her momma laughed, fanned her hand
Plum disappeared
shrank at the sound of his feet
the splat of bare skin on linoleum
as he skittered from her momma's bedroom
Plum hid in the gray light of the small screen
Behind her the bathroom door thudded open
a flick and a shaft of harsh yellow light intruded
the loud splash and pour as he emptied himself
She shriveled into the sofa's arm
eyes closed, cowering

4

Momma is asleep
the house is still
Plum retreats to the back porch
a pad of old newspapers
to guard against splinters and crooked nails
a fading sun, a book
the sweet summer night air
She trails her bare feet in the uncut grass
thick and green between her toes
the whisper of wind and insects
A sudden shadow's
slow searing press at her back
spongy pounding sounds
flood her ears; a hand at her neck
grips like his pinched words
All about her is noise
static and mayhem
strident and shrill
filling her throat, stealing
breath and words and sight
She clings to the rough
edge of the porch, a jagged nail
rigid like the rubber
baby doll her momma gave her
one Christmas
It is not my body, she begins
the ritual of severance
a hymn of redemption
Does not belong to me

Damp hands poke and pull
that girl, that body
hurting her with his
hammering and heavy
cruel like the knife
Momma uses to gut fish
She won't believe you, he says
And Plum knows he's right.

5

All about me is noise
I cower in crevices, shrinking
as static floods the air
shrill sounds
like knives sharpening
the scrape of steel against stone
or the endless screech of tires
before the crash
strident and shrill
It is not my body
does not belong to me
My feet are stumps
shoes flop about,
I cannot move
My blouse blows and floats like a garbage bag
a loose sack to conceal and dress wounds
My skin is raw with sweat and fear
but he does not see. He takes
Leaves the leftovers crumpled in corners
like dirty socks so he can find them again
to sniff before wearing one more time

6

I cannot see my feet
or hear Momma's screech
Her mouth is a round dark cave
with sharp teeth
Her eyes are angry, tired
and helpless
I smile up at her
but she grabs me
her fingers denting my arms
shaking me. Sounds like the rustle of garbage
sinking in its plastic sack
fill my ears. Its sick slickness
chafes my skin. Her nails dig deeper
as the maw opens and closes,
a chap lipped cavern
I can see waves of sound
They slip and slide down the black film
leaving trails of slime like snails
I watch them slither downwards
shiny mucus tracks on patent leather
My body is shaking again
Needles prick and pierce my arms
The maw grows wider and I close my eyes.

7

I squat over my jean jacket
layered in brown paper towels
bare feet crush the edges
careful to keep the center clean
babies shouldn't be born
to girls wearing shoes
the staggered hum of insects
streetlights slant
a thin ray across my knee
a yellow line on darkest brown
it plays, back and forth
shrinking and growing
company
a whoosh of wetness falls
from me
a slice of pain and need
I grunt
lean, my back low against the tiles
the smell of stale urine and worse
slips from under one of the stalls
my cheek against the cool white sink
like a hand offering comfort
the slice comes again, and need
gnawing asking demanding
I rest my arms on my haunches
and push, long and hard
nothing, a thin trail of blood
the cool pale hand on my forehead
as the slice cuts me again

the yellow line dances on the arm of my jacket
bits spill onto the floor, teasing
I want to laugh
but the slicing grabs hold
like a new surprise, loud and angry
the pale hand won't work
the yellow line stops and stares
I open my mouth to scream
but fear rules, teeth cut into my lip
blood, salty and sweet, seeps in
the need, and I am grunting on my haunches
pressure, low and eager,
pulling at my center
pinching and tugging, demanding
I push again, deep and strong
wanting it to stop
wanting to help, wanting
a whoosh of slop plops beneath me
lands wet, dark and stained
a lump of red, a splat darker spills again
covering and spilling and   relief
I lean into the cool hand

8

An eggplant with slick black hair
squirms and mewls in its glass cart
The maw is back
She doesn't want it or me
neither do I
Stiff white sheets and fluorescent lights
a void, a sterile cocoon
cool and blank like death
like emptiness, like silence
I pull the cover high over my head
and lie very still

9

Plum. A pretty girl touches my arm
She has new weave and a fresh dress
sixties, psychedelic, flower child print
a little jacket, like Michelle Obama
My eyes open to take her in
Warm eyes and straight teeth
educated by braces and Macy's lipstick
How're you feeling? Sunshine and welcome
make me want to smile, I don't
She pats my arm, opens a folder
and begins the post-mortem
Her pencil makes dents and dark marks
on the vanilla sheets, her voice a soothing draught
gathering answers that ooze and bubble like
toxins released by a fever. She still smiles
sad eyes and white teeth, for me
I nod and turn on my side
She pats my arm again
and leaves

10

Momma is angry at me
He is gone
She blames me
The police and social workers come
She blames me
They bring the baby, it cries
She blames me
Loud enough to wake the cadavers in the basement
She blames me
I cannot speak in her presence
I do not exist for her
I have never existed for her
She cries, wrings her hands
and blames me

11

The girl with the new weave says
I don't have to take it home
She asks what I want to do
I think of the sterile cocoon
I remember the splintered wood
on the back porch, the crooked nails
the feel of the hammer as it sank
into flesh and crushed bone
and I can't stop crying
The girl pats my back
rubs little circles ever so often
I lean my hip into the windowsill
We are a long way up
I imagine how it would feel to fall
to go thump onto the roof of the green Escalade
my body rag doll limp like in the movies, WHUMP!
But I know the windows don't open
Nurse says open windows confuse the ventilation system

12

Sing to me
Nobody ever sang to me
The candy striper is holding the eggplant
swaddled in pink flannel
Rocking her and singing
It sucks at the bottle and looks up
at the striper's mouth, a baby finger
reaching, trying to grab the song
like the voice is a good dream
Its lips puckered, jaws moving
like that milk, like life
is a brand new pair of Ecko Reds
Blanket clad eggplant over her shoulder,
she pats its back, bouncing to the little tune
I press my head against the glass partition
trying to get closer
trying to hear the song

13

Momma says, *You made your bed.*
She says, *You can't leave your blood with strangers.*
I listen and I don't
She cries a lot, but never says she's sorry
She asks God what she did
to deserve a daughter like me
I'm singing like India in my head
If you wanna a butterfly[2]
You gotta be a butterfly
I press my body into the cool white sheets
Still a swoon in a cocoon
I listen to the swish of my legs and arms
like the flutter of wings as they slide across the crispness
The new weave lady comes into the room
stands next to the bed, next to Momma
Lays her hand on mine, cool like the sheets,
shows a thin line of teeth
Momma glares at her, but the maw closes
She shows the line of teeth to Momma

---

[2] The following three italicized lines are from "Butterfly" by India Arie on her album *Acoustic Soul* produced by Motown, 2001.

14

She tried to make me take it
Momma did
Said I was a minor
had to do what she said
So the new weave lady
put me in this place
for safekeeping
The windows don't open here
either, but outside
sun and green grass
wait for me
Sometimes
I wonder about the eggplant
where it is
if anybody sings to her
if it's still wrapped in the pink flannel cocoon
But most times I just sit here
                              and ripen.

Sane Notes and Quick References
in alphabetical order

Bolsheviks (also Bolshevists): A faction of the Marxist Russian Social Democratic Labour Party, but generally those loyal to the communist revolutionary ideals of Trotsky

Boricua: The people of Puerto Rico

Borinquen (also Borikén): The indigenous Taíno name for the island of Puerto Rico

Cortés: Hernán Cortés, Spanish Conquistador, 1485-1547

gnarled witches: Used in "Lily," Poem 8, with a nod to Libyan poet, Khaled Mattawa, who planted this phrase in my head when he read in Detroit

Julia de Burgos: Puerto Rican born lyrical poet and revolutionary

Lolita Lebron: Puerto Rican nationalist imprisoned for her part in a 1954 shooting in the US House of Representatives

maw: "the throat, gullet, jaws, or oral cavity (of some voracious animals)" *Webster's New Universal Unabridged Dictionary*, 1983

Olga Viscal Garriga: A student leader/spokesperson of the Puerto Rican Nationalist Party

Taíno: Relative of the Arawak people of South America, the Taíno are the indigenous people of the Caribbean; *i.e.* Puerto Rico, Haiti, Cuba, *et al.*

The Pearl: Cuba has historically been referred to as "The Pearl of the Antilles." However, this phrase has been applied to other Caribbean islands. *La Perla* is also the slum that lies along the northern wall of Old San Juan in Puerto Rico.

Yuquiyu (also Yúcahu): Taíno god of creation who dwells in the sacred rain forest

About the Author

Esperanza Cintrón was born in Detroit, Michigan when it was a prime producer of music and automobiles and was the fifth largest city in the country with a population that exceeded 1.5 million. Her first book of poetry, *Chocolate City Latina*, published by Swank Press in 2005, is flavored with a bit of her African American and Boricua spice while exploring that late twentieth century metropolis "When Cadillacs Roamed the Midwest." The city's history and its people, especially the women, who lived through the highs and lows of the midwestern city-town permeate her work. *What Keeps Me Sane* is a series of four narrative cycle poems that examines the connections between sanity, survival, and self-image from the perspective of four women.

Cintrón studied film and communication, earning both bachelor's and master's degrees from Wayne State University and a doctorate in English literature from The State University of New York (SUNY) at Albany. As a component of her doctoral studies, she co-founded The Sisters of Color Writers Collective and its literary journal, *Seeds* (1989-2006), both of which were dedicated to publishing the works of women.

Her work, both poetry and short fiction, has been published in a number of anthologies including *Double-Stitch: Black Women Write About Mothers & Daughters* (Beacon Press), *Erotique Noir/Black Erotica* (Doubleday), *Abandon Automobile* (Wayne State University Press), and the journals *Capirotada, 13th Moon,* and *The Little Magazine.*

She has been the recipient of a Michigan Council for the Arts Individual Artist grant and the *Metro Times* Poetry Prize. She was a 2012 Callaloo Creative Writing Fellow.

The mother of one daughter who is a student at The University of Michigan, Cintrón currently lives, writes, and teaches college in downtown Detroit.

71